Dressing Pretty Fashion Doll™

Plastic Canvas

2

4

6

8

11

11

13

9

10

12

14

Doll

Size: **Doll (on stand):** 5½ inches W x 15 inches H
(14cm x 38.1cm)
Skill Level: Intermediate

Materials

- ❏ 2 sheets 7-count plastic canvas
- ❏ Needloft® craft yarn as listed in color key
- ❏ 6-strand embroidery floss as listed in color key
- ❏ #16 tapestry needle
- ❏ Blond curly doll hair
- ❏ 1¼ inches (3.8cm) hook-and-loop fastener
- ❏ 2 (6 x ¾-inch/15.2 x 1.9cm) jumbo craft sticks
- ❏ Craft glue and hot-glue gun

Cutting & Stitching

1 Cut two doll pieces from plastic canvas according to graph. One piece will remain unstitched.

2 Stitch remaining piece following graph, working uncoded areas with fleshtone Continental Stitches.

3 When background stitching is completed, work embroidery with 6-strand embroidery floss, working **Fly Stitch** (see illustration) for upper lip on mouth.

4 Place unstitched piece behind stitched piece with craft sticks between, one on top of the other. Whipstitch together following graph.

5 Cut doll hair in desired lengths. Fold lengths in half. Use hot glue to attach to head as desired. Trim to desired length as needed.

6 Cut rough side of hook-and-loop fastener in half so there are two ⅝-inch lengths. Cut each of these in half lengthwise. Glue two strips above bathing suit to resemble straps, trimming as needed to fit. Glue one rough-side strip to white stitching between legs.

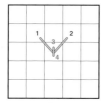

Fly Stitch

Hook-and-loop fastener

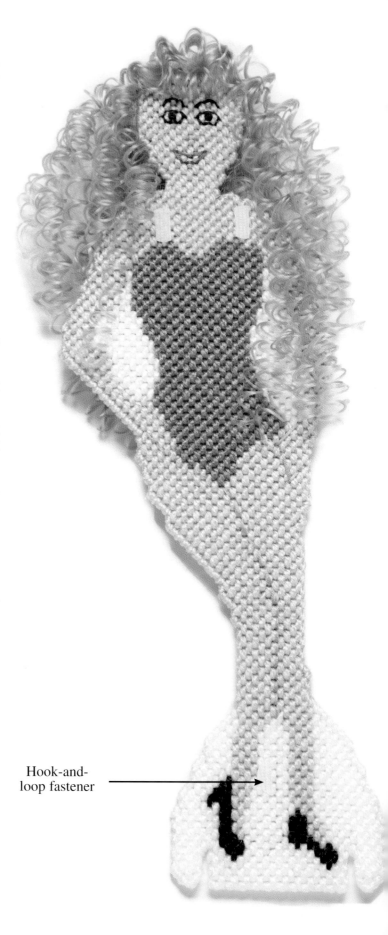

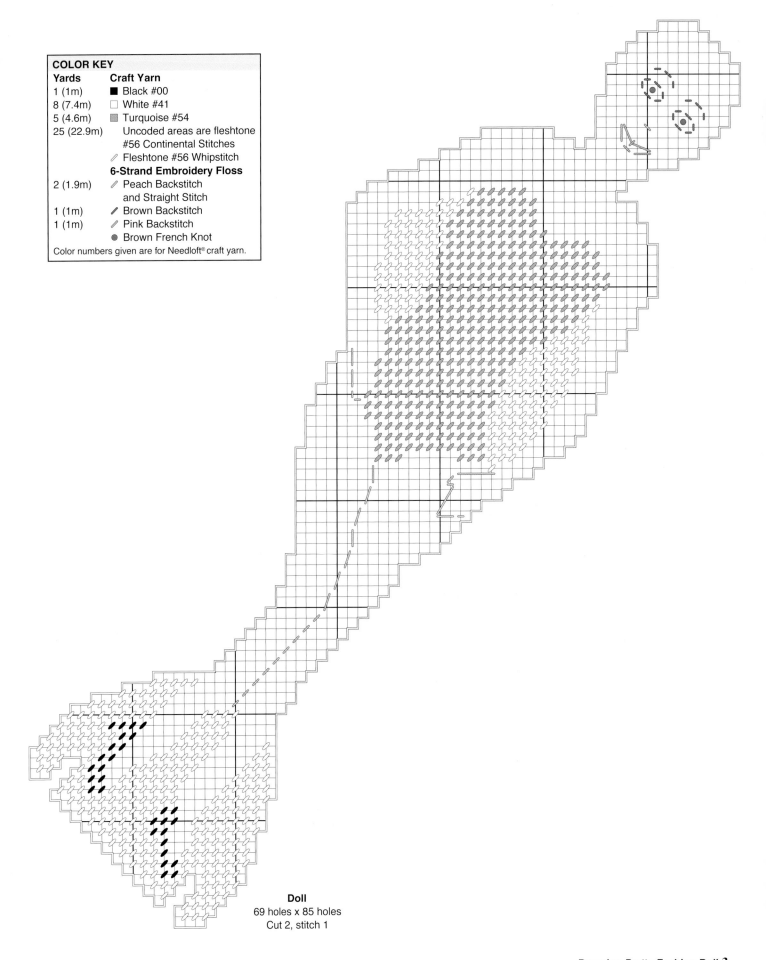

COLOR KEY

Yards	Craft Yarn
1 (1m)	■ Black #00
8 (7.4m)	□ White #41
5 (4.6m)	▨ Turquoise #54
25 (22.9m)	Uncoded areas are fleshtone #56 Continental Stitches
	⟋ Fleshtone #56 Whipstitch

6-Strand Embroidery Floss

2 (1.9m)	⟋ Peach Backstitch and Straight Stitch
1 (1m)	⟋ Brown Backstitch
1 (1m)	⟋ Pink Backstitch
	● Brown French Knot

Color numbers given are for Needloft® craft yarn.

Doll
69 holes x 85 holes
Cut 2, stitch 1

Doll Stand

Size: 2⅝ inches W x 6⅜ inches H x 3⅛ inches D
(6.7cm x 16.2cm x 7.9cm)
Skill Level: Intermediate

Materials

- ❏ 1 sheet 7-count plastic canvas
- ❏ Needloft® craft yarn as listed in color key
- ❏ #16 tapestry needle
- ❏ ¼ cup pebbles

Cutting & Stitching

1 Cut plastic canvas according to graphs (page 5). One brace will remain unstitched.

2 Stitch top, front, back and base as graphed, leaving uncoded area on base unstitched.

3 Stitch one brace following graph. Reverse second brace and work stitches in reverse. Place stitched braces with wrong sides together, sandwiching unstitched brace between. Whipstitch three pieces together along side and top edges from blue dot to blue dot, leaving bottom edges unworked at this time.

4 For one side, place two pieces together and stitch as one following graph. Reverse remaining two sides; place together and stitch as one, working stitches in reverse.

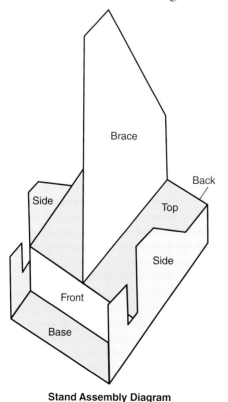

Stand Assembly Diagram

Assembly

1 Following assembly diagram and graphs, Whipstitch front and back to top. Stitch brace to top where indicated. Whipstitch sides to front, back and top.

2 Whipstitch base to front and sides. Fill back part of stand with pebbles; Whipstitch closed. Overcast remaining edges.

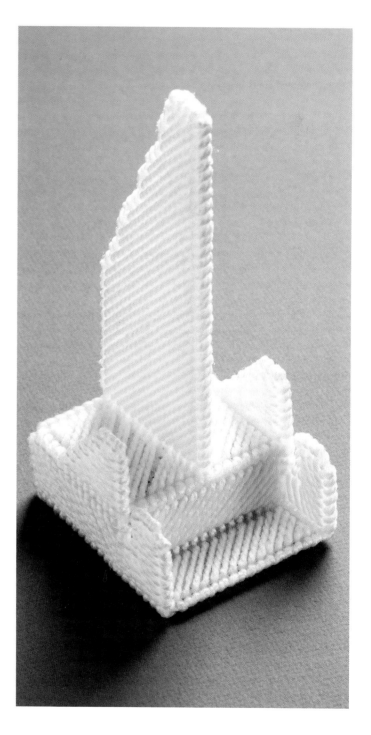

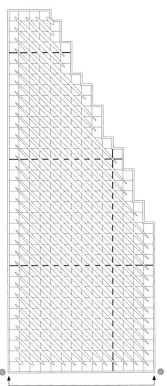

Whipstitch to top

Brace
14 holes x 34 holes
Cut 3
Stitch 1 as graphed
Reverse 1 and work
stitches in reverse
Do not stitch remaining brace

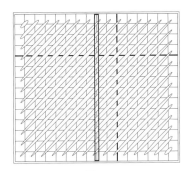

Top
16 holes x 14 holes
Cut 1

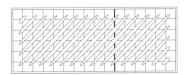

Front & Back
16 holes x 6 holes
Cut 2

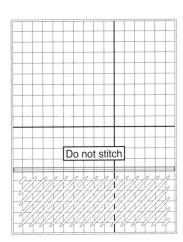

Do not stitch

Base
16 holes x 20 holes
Cut 1

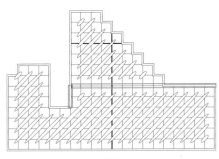

Side
20 holes x 13 holes
Cut 4
Place 2 together; stitch as 1 following graph
Reverse 2 and place together;
stitch as 1 working stitches in reverse

Evening Gown

Size: 6 inches W x 11¼ inches H
(15.2cm x 28.6cm)
Skill Level: Intermediate

Materials

❏ 1 sheet 7-count plastic canvas
❏ Needloft® craft yarn as listed in color key
❏ #16 tapestry needle
❏ 4 inches (10.2cm) 4mm prestrung pearls
❏ ¼ yard (0.2m) pink satin ribbon
❏ 3 (⅝-inch/1.6cm) round hook-and-loop fasteners
❏ Craft glue or hot-glue gun

Cutting & Stitching

1 Cut evening gown from plastic canvas according to graph.

2 Stitch and Overcast piece following graph, working uncoded areas with purple Continental Stitches.

3 Using photo as a guide, cut a 2-inch (5.1cm) length of ribbon and glue to waist. Tie remaining ribbon in a bow and glue to ribbon on waist, trimming ends as desired. Glue pearls to neck area.

4 Glue soft side of hook-and-loop fasteners to back of gown, aligning with hook-and-loop tape on doll.

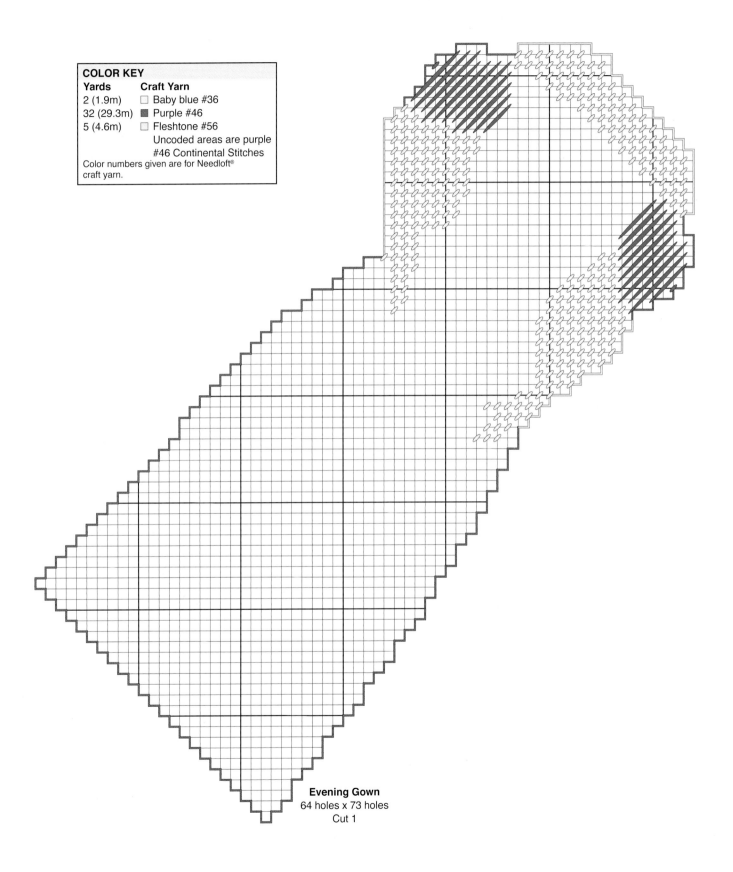

COLOR KEY

Yards	Craft Yarn
2 (1.9m)	☐ Baby blue #36
32 (29.3m)	■ Purple #46
5 (4.6m)	☐ Fleshtone #56

Uncoded areas are purple
#46 Continental Stitches
Color numbers given are for Needloft®
craft yarn.

Evening Gown
64 holes x 73 holes
Cut 1

Dressing Pretty Fashion Doll 7

Overalls

Size: 4¾ inches W x 10⅜ inches H
(12.1cm x 26.4cm)
Skill Level: Intermediate

Materials

❏ 1 sheet 7-count plastic canvas
❏ Needloft® craft yarn as listed in color key
❏ #16 tapestry needle
❏ 3 (⅝-inch/1.6cm) round hook-and-loop fasteners
❏ Craft glue or hot-glue gun

Cutting & Stitching

1 Cut overalls from plastic canvas according to graph.

2 Stitch and Overcast piece following graph, working Continental Stitches in uncoded areas as follows: white background with royal blue, green background with mermaid.

3 Glue soft side of hook-and-loop fasteners to back of overalls, aligning with hook-and-loop tape on doll.

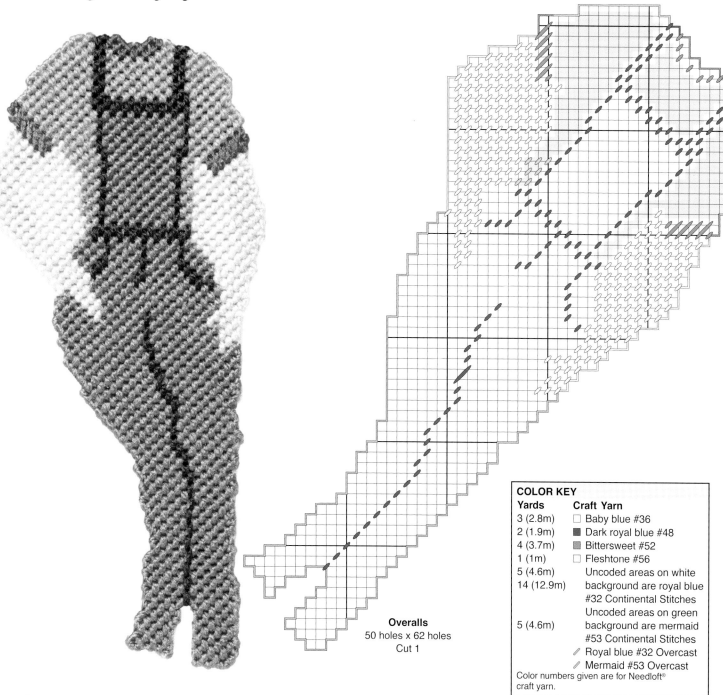

Overalls
50 holes x 62 holes
Cut 1

COLOR KEY

Yards	Craft Yarn
3 (2.8m)	☐ Baby blue #36
2 (1.9m)	■ Dark royal blue #48
4 (3.7m)	▨ Bittersweet #52
1 (1m)	☐ Fleshtone #56
5 (4.6m)	Uncoded areas on white
14 (12.9m)	background are royal blue #32 Continental Stitches
5 (4.6m)	Uncoded areas on green background are mermaid #53 Continental Stitches
	⁄ Royal blue #32 Overcast
	⁄ Mermaid #53 Overcast

Color numbers given are for Needloft® craft yarn.

Shorts Outfit

Size: 4¾ inches W x 6⅞ inches H
(12.1cm x 17.5cm)
Skill Level: Intermediate

Materials

❑ ½ sheet 7-count plastic canvas
❑ Needloft® craft yarn as listed in color key
❑ #16 tapestry needle
❑ 2 (⅝-inch/1.6cm) round hook-and-loop fasteners
❑ Craft glue or hot-glue gun

Cutting & Stitching

1 Cut shorts outfit from plastic canvas according to graph.

2 Stitch and Overcast piece following graph, working Continental Stitches in uncoded areas as follows: burgundy background with burgundy, beige background with camel, white background with fleshtone.

3 Glue soft side of hook-and-loop fasteners to back of overalls at shoulders, aligning with hook-and-loop tape on doll.

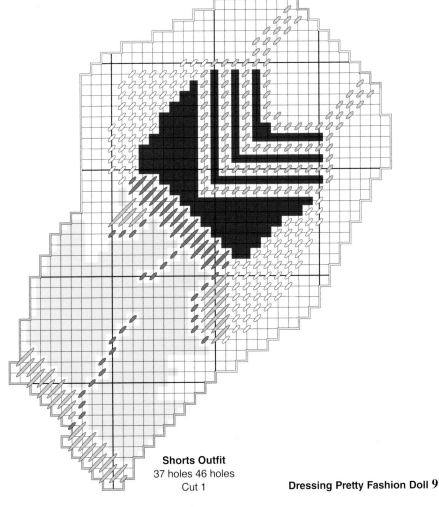

COLOR KEY	
Yards	**Craft Yarn**
2 (1.9m)	▨ Lavender #05
2 (1.9m)	■ Cinnamon #14
3 (2.8m)	☐ Baby blue #36
6 (5.5m)	▨ Camel #43
3 (2.8m)	Uncoded areas on burgundy background are burgundy #03 Continental Stitches
	Uncoded areas on beige background are camel #43 Continental Stitches
6 (5.5m)	Uncoded areas on white background are fleshtone #56 Continental Stitches
	⁄ Camel #43 Overcast
	⁄ Fleshtone #56 Overcast
Color numbers given are for Needloft® craft yarn.	

Shorts Outfit
37 holes 46 holes
Cut 1

Mini Dress

Size: 4¾ inches W x 7 inches H (12.1cm x 17.8cm)
Skill Level: Intermediate

Materials

❏ ¼ sheet 7-count plastic canvas
❏ Needloft® craft yarn as listed in color key
❏ #16 tapestry needle
❏ 2 (⅝-inch/1.6cm) round hook-and-loop fasteners
❏ Craft glue or hot-glue gun

Cutting & Stitching

1 Cut mini dress from plastic canvas according to graph.

2 Stitch and Overcast piece following graph, working Continental Stitches in uncoded areas as follows: white background with watermelon, yellow background with yellow.

3 Glue soft side of hook-and-loop fasteners to back of dress at shoulders, aligning with hook-and-loop tape on doll.

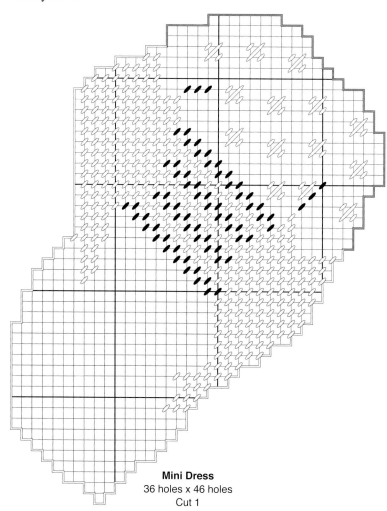

Mini Dress
36 holes x 46 holes
Cut 1

COLOR KEY

Yards	Craft Yarn
2 (1.9m)	■ Black #00
3 (2.8m)	☐ Baby blue #36
2 (1.9m)	☐ White #41
3 (2.8m)	☐ Fleshtone #56
5 (4.6m)	Uncoded areas on white background are watermelon #55 Continental Stitches
6 (5.5m)	Uncoded areas on yellow background are yellow #57 Continental Stitches
	⁄ Watermelon #55 Overcast
	⁄ Yellow #57 Overcast

Color numbers given are for Needloft® craft yarn.

Hat

Size: 3½ inches W x 2¼ inches H (8.9cm x 5.7cm)
Skill Level: Intermediate

Materials

❑ Small amount 7-count plastic canvas
❑ Needloft® craft yarn as listed in color key
❑ #16 tapestry needle

Cutting & Stitching

1 Cut hat from plastic canvas according to graph, cutting out hole as indicated. Cut plastic canvas apart where indicated at blue line.

2 Stitch and Overcast piece following graph.

Shoulder Bag

Size: 1¾ inches W x 6⅛ inches H (4.4cm x 15.6cm)
Skill Level: Intermediate

Materials

❑ ¼ sheet 7-count plastic canvas
❑ Needloft® craft yarn as listed in color key
❑ #16 tapestry needle

Cutting & Stitching

1 Cut shoulder bag from plastic canvas according to graph.

2 Stitch piece following graph.

3 Overcast edges; Whipstitch top edges of handle together.

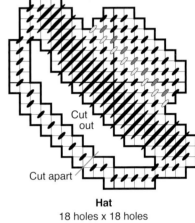

COLOR KEY

Yards	Craft Yarn
6 (5.5m)	■ Black #00
1 (1m)	▨ Watermelon #55
1 (1m)	☐ Yellow #57

Color numbers given are for Needloft® craft yarn.

Hat
18 holes x 18 holes
Cut 1

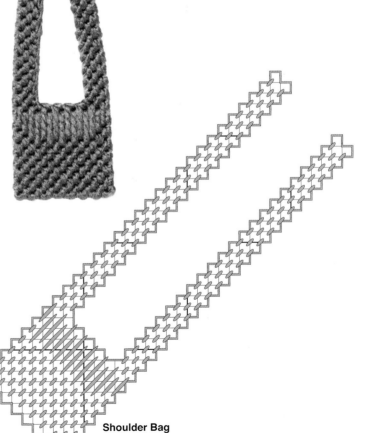

COLOR KEY

Yards	Craft Yarn
10 (9.2m)	▨ Maple #13

Color number given is for Needloft® craft yarn.

Shoulder Bag
36 holes x 36 holes
Cut 1

Party Dress

Size: 4¾ inches W x 5⅞ inches H (12.1cm x 15cm)
Skill Level: Intermediate

Materials

❏ ¼ sheet 7-count plastic canvas
❏ Needloft® craft yarn as listed in color key
❏ #16 tapestry needle
❏ 4 inches (12.1cm) 4mm prestrung pearls
❏ 1-inch (25mm) white ribbon bow with pearl center
❏ 3 (⅝-inch/1.6cm) round hook-and-loop fasteners
❏ Craft glue or hot-glue gun

Cutting & Stitching

1 Cut party dress from plastic canvas according to graph.

2 Stitch and Overcast piece following graph, working Continental Stitches in uncoded areas with fleshtone.

3 Using photo as a guide, glue pearls to neck area. Glue ribbon bow to waist.

4 Glue soft side of two hook-and-loop fasteners to back of dress at shoulders, aligning with hook-and-loop tape on doll. Cut rough side of one fastener to fit hand on left side; glue in place. *Note: Use remaining soft side of fastener on back of clutch purse.*

5 Place clutch purse over hand where indicated with blue lines.

COLOR KEY	
Yards	**Craft Yarn**
9 (8.3m)	■ Christmas red #02
3 (2.8m)	☐ Baby blue #36
1 (1m)	☐ White #41
6 (5.5m)	Uncoded area is fleshtone #56 Continental Stitches
	⁄ Fleshtone #56 Overcast
	☐ Attach purse

Color numbers given are for Needloft® craft yarn.

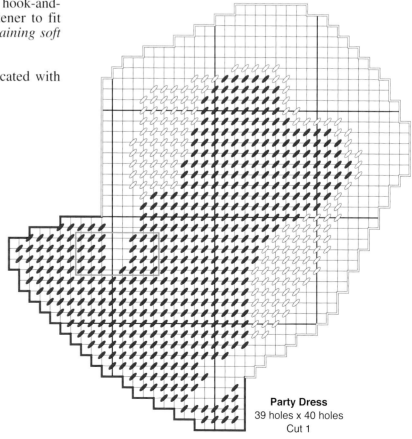

Party Dress
39 holes x 40 holes
Cut 1